U.S. Department
of Transportation

**Federal Aviation
Administration**

MW00803283

Remote Pilot – Small Unmanned Aircraft Systems

Airman Certification Standards

April 2021

**Flight Standards Service
Washington, DC 20591**

Acknowledgments

The U.S. Department of Transportation, Federal Aviation Administration (FAA), Office of Safety Standards, Regulatory Support Division, Airman Testing Branch, P.O. Box 25082, Oklahoma City, OK 73125 developed this Airman Certification Standards (ACS) document with the assistance of the subject matter experts in the area related to small Unmanned Aircraft Systems (UAS).

Availability

This ACS is available for download from www.faa.gov. Please send comments regarding this document using the following link to the Airman Testing Branch mailbox: AFS630Comments@faa.gov.

Material in FAA-S-ACS-10B is effective April 6, 2021.

Foreword

The Federal Aviation Administration (FAA) publishes the Remote Pilot – small Unmanned Aircraft Systems (UAS) Airman Certification Standards (ACS) document to communicate a means to evaluate the aeronautical knowledge standards for certification knowledge testing for a Remote Pilot Certificate with a small UAS rating.

The FAA views the ACS as the foundation of its transition to a more integrated and systematic approach to airman certification. The ACS is part of the Safety Management System (SMS) framework that the FAA uses to mitigate risks associated with airman certification training and testing. Specifically, the ACS, associated guidance, and test question components of the airman certification system are constructed around the four functional components of an SMS:

- Safety Policy that defines and describes aeronautical knowledge, risk management, and flight proficiency as integrated components of the airman certification system;

- Safety Risk Management processes through which both internal and external stakeholders identify changes in regulations, safety recommendations, or other factors. These changes are then evaluated to determine whether they require modification of airman testing and training materials;

- Safety Assurance processes to ensure the prompt and appropriate incorporation of changes arising from new regulations and safety recommendations; and

- Safety Promotion in the form of ongoing engagement with both external stakeholders (e.g., the aviation training community) and FAA policy divisions.

Rick Domingo
Executive Director, Flight Standards Service

Revision History

Document	Description	Revision Date
FAA-S-ACS-10	Remote Pilot – Small Unmanned Aircraft Systems Airman Certification Standards	July 2016
FAA-S-ACS-10A	Remote Pilot – Small Unmanned Aircraft Systems (Certification and Recurrent Knowledge Testing) Airman Certification Standards	June 2018
FAA-S-ACS-10B	Remote Pilot – Small Unmanned Aircraft Systems Airman Certification Standards	April 2021

Major Enhancements to Version FAA-S-ACS-10B

Section	Action	Description
Introduction	Updated	"Airman Certification Standards Concept" subsection
	Updated	Using the ACS subsection
References	Updated	Task references, as necessary
Area of Operation I, Regulations	Added	Knowledge elements K6, K7, and K8 to Task A, General
	Added	Knowledge elements K23, K24, K25, K26, K27, and K28 to Task B, Operating Rules
	Added	Task E, Operations Over People
	Added	Task F, Remote Identification (RID)
Area of Operation II, Airspace Classification and Operating Requirements	Added	Knowledge elements K6, K7, K8, K9, and K10 to Task B, Airspace Operational Requirements
Area of Operation V, Operations	Added	Knowledge element K8 to Task B, Airport Operations
	Added	Knowledge elements K6 and K7 to Task C, Emergency Procedures
	Added	Knowledge elements K8 and K9 to Task E, Physiology
	Added	Knowledge elements K6 and K7 to Task F, Maintenance and Inspection Procedures
Appendices	Updated	Appendix 1: Certification Knowledge Test, Eligibility, and Testing Centers
	Updated	Appendix 3: Airman Knowledge Test Report for Certification
	Updated	Appendix 4: References

Table of Contents

Introduction

Airman Certification Standards Concept

The goal of the airman certification process is to ensure the applicant possesses knowledge consistent with the privileges of the Remote Pilot Certificate with a small Unmanned Aircraft Systems (sUAS) rating, as well as the ability to manage the risks of flight in order to act as a remote pilot-in-command (PIC).

In fulfilling its responsibilities for the airman certification process, the Federal Aviation Administration (FAA) Flight Standards Service (AFS) plans, develops, and maintains materials related to airman certification testing. These materials include several components. The FAA knowledge test measures mastery of the aeronautical knowledge areas listed in Title 14 of the Code of Federal Regulations (14 CFR) parts 89 and 107. Other materials, such as airman knowledge testing supplements in the FAA-CT-8080 series and FAA online training, provide guidance to applicants on aeronautical knowledge and risk management.

The FAA recognizes that safe operations in today's complex National Airspace System (NAS) require a more systematic integration of aeronautical knowledge and risk management. The FAA further recognizes the need to more clearly calibrate knowledge and risk management to the level of the Remote Pilot Certificate with an sUAS rating.

The ACS integrates the elements of knowledge and risk management in 14 CFR parts 89 and 107 for a Remote Pilot Certificate with an sUAS rating. It thus forms the comprehensive standard for what an applicant knows and considers to successfully complete each Task tested on the knowledge test.

In keeping with this integrated and systematic approach, the knowledge Task elements of each Task identify what the applicant should know and understand for sUAS operations conducted under 14 CFR parts 89 and 107. The applicant demonstrates this understanding by passing the knowledge test.

Using the ACS

This Remote Pilot ACS includes Areas of Operation and Tasks for the issuance of a Remote Pilot Certificate with an sUAS rating in accordance with 14 CFR part 107, section 107.65.

Element codes in the ACS divide into four components. For example:

UA.I.B.K10:
> **UA** = ACS (Unmanned Aircraft Systems)
> **I** = Area of Operation (Regulations)
> **B** = Task (Operating Rules)
> **K10** = Knowledge Element (Visual line of sight (VLOS) aircraft operations.)

At the conclusion of a knowledge test, an applicant is given their Knowledge Test Report (KTR). The KTR lists the applicant's name, date of the test, the type of test, a unique test identification number, the score and ACS Codes for questions that were answered incorrectly. The printed ACS Codes guides the applicant to the area(s) that were found to be deficient in the test. The codes are found in this Airman Certification Standards document.

The FAA encourages applicants to use this ACS as a reference while preparing for the certification airman knowledge test. The FAA revises this ACS as circumstances require.

For those applicants who do not pass the knowledge test for certification, remedial instruction and an endorsement from an instructor is not required for retesting. See Appendix 1: Certification Knowledge Tests, Eligibility, and Testing Centers for details on passing the Unmanned Aircraft General – Small (UAG) certification airman knowledge test.

I. Regulations

Task A. General

References	*14 CFR parts 89 and 107, subpart A; AC 107-2; FAA-H-8083-25; FAA-G-8082-22*
Objective	*To determine that the applicant is knowledgeable in the general regulatory requirements of 14 CFR parts 89 and 107.*
Knowledge	*The applicant demonstrates understanding of:*
UA.I.A.K1	Applicability of 14 CFR part 107 to small unmanned aircraft operations.
UA.I.A.K2	Definitions used in 14 CFR part 107.
UA.I.A.K3	The ramifications of falsification, reproduction, or alteration of a certificate, rating, authorization, record, or report.
UA.I.A.K4	Accident reporting.
UA.I.A.K5	Inspection, testing, and demonstration of compliance.
UA.I.A.K6	Multiple category sUAS.
UA.I.A.K7	Record retention.
UA.I.A.K8	Previously manufactured sUAS.
Risk Management	*[Reserved]*
Skills	*[Not Applicable]*

I. Regulations

Task B. Operating Rules

References	*14 CFR parts 47, 48, 89, and 107, subpart B; AC 107-2; FAA-H-8083-25; FAA-G-8082-22*
Objective	*To determine that the applicant is knowledgeable of the operating rules of 14 CFR parts 89 and 107, the registration rules of 14 CFR parts 47 and 48, and other associated operating requirements.*
Knowledge	*The applicant demonstrates understanding of:*

UA.I.B.K1	Registration requirements for sUAS.
UA.I.B.K2	Requirement for the sUAS to be in a condition for safe operation.
UA.I.B.K3	Medical condition(s) that would interfere with safe operation of an sUAS.
UA.I.B.K4	Responsibility and authority of the remote PIC.
UA.I.B.K4a	a. Allowing a person other than the remote PIC to manipulate the flight controls
UA.I.B.K5	Regulatory deviation and reporting requirements for in-flight emergencies.
UA.I.B.K6	Hazardous operations.
UA.I.B.K6a	a. Careless or reckless
UA.I.B.K6b	b. Dropping an object
UA.I.B.K7	Operating from a moving aircraft or moving land- or water-borne vehicle.
UA.I.B.K8	Alcohol or drugs and the provisions on prohibition of use.
UA.I.B.K9	Daylight operations.
UA.I.B.K10	Visual line of sight (VLOS) aircraft operations.
UA.I.B.K11	Requirements when a visual observer is used.
UA.I.B.K12	Prohibition of operating multiple sUAS.
UA.I.B.K13	Prohibition of carrying hazardous material.
UA.I.B.K14	Staying safely away from other aircraft and right-of-way rules.
UA.I.B.K14a	a. See and avoid other aircraft and other potential hazard considerations of the remote PIC
UA.I.B.K15	Operations over human beings (Refer to Area of Operation I, Task E).
UA.I.B.K16	Prior authorization required for operation in certain airspace.
UA.I.B.K17	Operating in the vicinity of airports.
UA.I.B.K18	Operating in prohibited or restricted areas.
UA.I.B.K19	Flight restrictions in the proximity of certain areas designated by notice to airmen (NOTAM).
UA.I.B.K20	Preflight familiarization, inspection, and actions for aircraft operations.
UA.I.B.K21	Operating limitations for sUAS.
UA.I.B.K21a	a. Maximum groundspeed
UA.I.B.K21b	b. Altitude limitations
UA.I.B.K21c	c. Minimum visibility
UA.I.B.K21d	d. Cloud clearance requirements
UA.I.B.K22	Requirements for a Remote Pilot Certificate with an sUAS rating.
UA.I.B.K23	Automated operations.

UA.I.B.K24	Civil twilight operations.	
UA.I.B.K25	Night operations.	
UA.I.B.K26	Transportation of property.	
UA.I.B.K27	ATC transponder equipment prohibition.	
UA.I.B.K28	ADS-B Out prohibition.	
Risk Management	*[Reserved]*	
Skills	*[Not Applicable]*	

I. Regulations

Task C. Remote Pilot Certification with an sUAS Rating

References	*14 CFR part 107, subpart C; AC 107-2; FAA-H-8083-25; FAA-G-8082-22*
Objective	*To determine that the applicant is knowledgeable in the requirements associated with remote pilot certification with an sUAS rating.*
Knowledge	*The applicant demonstrates understanding of:*
UA.I.C.K1	Offenses involving alcohol or drugs.
UA.I.C.K2	The consequences of refusing to submit to a drug or alcohol test or to furnish test results.
UA.I.C.K3	The eligibility requirements for a Remote Pilot Certificate with an sUAS rating.
UA.I.C.K4	Aeronautical knowledge recency.
Risk Management	*[Reserved]*
Skills	*[Not Applicable]*

I. Regulations

Task D. Waivers

References	*14 CFR part 107, subpart D; AC 107-2; FAA-H-8083-25; FAA-G-8082-22*
Objective	*To determine that the applicant is knowledgeable of the FAA waiver policy and requirements.*
Knowledge	*The applicant demonstrates understanding of:*
UA.I.D.K1	Waiver policy and requirements.
Risk Management	*[Reserved]*
Skills	*[Not Applicable]*

I. Regulations

Task E. Operations Over People

References	*14 CFR parts 89 and 107; AC 107-2; FAA-H-8083-25; FAA-G-8082-22*
Objective	*To determine that the applicant is knowledgeable of the operating rules of 14 CFR parts 89 and 107, and the associated operating requirements when operating over people.*
Knowledge	*The applicant demonstrates understanding of:*
UA.I.E.K1	Remote pilot responsibilities when operating over people.
UA.I.E.K2	Operations over people at night.
UA.I.E.K3	Category of operations, including:
UA.I.E.K3a	a. Category 1
UA.I.E.K3b	b. Category 2
UA.I.E.K3c	c. Category 3
UA.I.E.K3d	d. Category 4
UA.I.E.K4	Selecting an operational area.
UA.I.E.K5	Minimum distances from a person.
UA.I.E.K6	Operations over moving vehicles.
UA.I.E.K7	Modifications to an sUAS.
UA.I.E.K8	Closed and restricted access sites.
UA.I.E.K9	Remote Pilot operating instructions.
UA.I.E.K10	Required components and Category declaration.
UA.I.E.K11	Optional components.
UA.I.E.K12	Applicant produced, designed, or modified sUAS for operations over people.
UA.I.E.K13	Declaration of Compliance (DoC).
UA.I.E.K14	Maintenance of an sUAS that is eligible for operations over people.
UA.I.E.K15	Means of Compliance (MoC).
UA.I.E.K16	Impact kinetic energy.
UA.I.E.K17	Exposed rotating parts.
Risk Management	*[Reserved]*
Skills	*[Not Applicable]*

I. Regulations

Task F. Remote Identification (RID)

References	*14 CFR part 89; AC 107-2; FAA-H-8083-25; FAA-G-8082-22*
Objective	*To determine the applicant exhibits satisfactory knowledge associated with operating rules of 14 CFR part 89 and their associated operating requirements.*
Knowledge	*The applicant demonstrates understanding of:*
UA.I.F.K1	Standard remote identification.
UA.I.F.K2	Alternative remote identification.
UA.I.F.K3	Operations for aeronautical research.
UA.I.F.K4	ADS-B Out.
UA.I.F.K5	Confirmation of identification.
UA.I.F.K6	Minimum message elements broadcast for remote identification.
UA.I.F.K7	Product labeling.
Risk Management	*[Reserved]*
Skills	*[Not Applicable]*

II. Airspace Classification and Operating Requirements
Task A. Airspace Classification

References	*14 CFR part 71; AC 107-2; AIM; FAA-H-8083-25; FAA-G-8082-22*
Objective	*To determine that the applicant is knowledgeable in airspace classification.*
Knowledge	*The applicant demonstrates understanding of:*
UA.II.A.K1	General airspace:
UA.II.A.K1a	a. Class B controlled airspace
UA.II.A.K1b	b. Class C controlled airspace
UA.II.A.K1c	c. Class D controlled airspace
UA.II.A.K1d	d. Class E controlled airspace
UA.II.A.K1e	e. Class G uncontrolled airspace
UA.II.A.K2	Special-use airspace, such as prohibited, restricted, warning areas, military operation areas, alert areas, and controlled firing areas.
UA.II.A.K3	Other airspace areas, such as Airport Advisory Services, Military Training Routes (MTRs), Temporary Flight Restrictions (TFRs), Parachute Jump Operations, Terminal Radar Service Areas (TRSAs), National Security Areas (NSA) and Visual Flight Rules (VFR) routes.
UA.II.A.K4	Air Traffic Control (ATC) and the NAS.
Risk Management	*[Reserved]*
Skills	*[Not Applicable]*

II. Airspace Classification and Operating Requirements
Task B. Airspace Operational Requirements

References	*14 CFR part 71; AC 107-2; AIM; FAA-H-8083-25; FAA-G-8082-22; SAFO 10015*
Objective	*To determine that the applicant is knowledgeable of airspace operational requirements.*
Knowledge	*The applicant demonstrates understanding of:*
UA.II.B.K1	Basic weather minimums.
UA.II.B.K2	ATC authorizations and related operating limitations.
UA.II.B.K3	Operations near airports.
UA.II.B.K4	Potential flight hazards.
UA.II.B.K4a	a. Common aircraft accident causal factors
UA.II.B.K4b	b. Avoid flight beneath unmanned balloons
UA.II.B.K4c	c. Emergency airborne inspection of other aircraft
UA.II.B.K4d	d. Precipitation static
UA.II.B.K4e	e. Light amplification by stimulated emission of radiation (laser) operations and reporting illumination of aircraft
UA.II.B.K4f	f. Avoiding flight in the vicinity of thermal plumes such as smoke stacks and cooling towers
UA.II.B.K4g	g. Flying in the wire environment
UA.II.B.K5	The NOTAM system, including how to obtain an established NOTAM through Flight Service.
UA.II.B.K6	Operator equipment for night flight.
UA.II.B.K7	Ground structures and ground structure lighting.
UA.II.B.K8	Hazards on the ground that do not have lighting.
UA.II.B.K9	Manned aircraft lighting.
UA.II.B.K10	sUAS lighting requirements.
Risk Management	*[Reserved]*
Skills	*[Not Applicable]*

III. Weather

Task A. Sources of Weather

References	*AC 107-2; AIM; FAA-H-8083-25; FAA-G-8082-22*
Objective	*To determine that the applicant is knowledgeable in sources of weather information.*
Knowledge	*The applicant demonstrates understanding of:*
UA.III.A.K1	Internet weather briefing and sources of weather available for flight planning purposes.
UA.III.A.K2	Aviation routine weather reports (METAR).
UA.III.A.K3	Terminal aerodrome forecasts (TAF).
UA.III.A.K4	Weather charts.
UA.III.A.K5	Automated surface observing systems (ASOS) and automated weather observing systems (AWOS).
Risk Management	*[Reserved]*
Skills	*[Not Applicable]*

III. Weather

Task B. Effects of Weather on Performance

References	AC 107-2; AIM; FAA-H-8083-25; FAA-G-8082-22
Objective	To determine that the applicant is knowledgeable of the effects of weather on performance.
Knowledge	The applicant demonstrates understanding of:
UA.III.B.K1	Weather factors and their effects on performance.
UA.III.B.K1a	a. Density altitude
UA.III.B.K1b	b. Wind and currents
UA.III.B.K1c	c. Atmospheric stability, pressure, and temperature
UA.III.B.K1d	d. Air masses and fronts
UA.III.B.K1e	e. Thunderstorms and microbursts
UA.III.B.K1f	f. Tornadoes
UA.III.B.K1g	g. Icing
UA.III.B.K1h	h. Hail
UA.III.B.K1i	i. Fog
UA.III.B.K1j	j. Ceiling and visibility
UA.III.B.K1k	k. Lightning
Risk Management	[Reserved]
Skills	[Not Applicable]

IV. Loading and Performance

Task A. Loading and Performance

References	*AC 107-2; FAA-H-8083-25; FAA-G-8082-22*
Objective	*To determine that the applicant is knowledgeable in the loading and performance of an sUAS.*
Knowledge	*The applicant demonstrates understanding of:*
UA.IV.A.K1	General loading and performance, including:
UA.IV.A.K1a	a. Effects of loading changes
UA.IV.A.K1b	b. Balance, stability, and center of gravity
UA.IV.A.K2	Importance and use of performance data to calculate the effect on the aircraft's performance of an sUAS.
Risk Management	*[Reserved]*
Skills	*[Not Applicable]*

V. Operations

Task A. Radio Communications Procedures

References	*AC 107-2; AIM; FAA-H-8083-25; FAA-G-8082-22*
Objective	*To determine that the applicant is knowledgeable in radio communication procedures.*
Knowledge	*The applicant demonstrates understanding of:*
UA.V.A.K1	Airport operations with and without an operating control tower.
UA.V.A.K2	The description and use of a Common Traffic Advisory Frequency (CTAF) to monitor manned aircraft communications.
UA.V.A.K3	Recommended traffic advisory procedures used by manned aircraft pilots such as self-announcing of position and intentions.
UA.V.A.K4	Aeronautical advisory communication station (UNICOM) and associated communication procedures used by manned aircraft pilots.
UA.V.A.K5	Automatic Terminal Information Service (ATIS).
UA.V.A.K6	Aircraft call signs and registration numbers.
UA.V.A.K7	The phonetic alphabet.
UA.V.A.K8	Phraseology: altitudes, directions, speed, and time.
Risk Management	*[Reserved]*
Skills	*[Not Applicable]*

V. Operations

Task B. Airport Operations

References	*AC 107-2, 150/5200-32; AIM; FAA-H-8083-25; FAA-G-8082-22*
Objective	*To determine that the applicant is knowledgeable in airport operations.*
Knowledge	*The applicant demonstrates understanding of:*
UA.V.B.K1	Types of airports such as towered, uncontrolled towered, heliport, and seaplane bases.
UA.V.B.K2	ATC towers, such as ensuring the remote pilot can monitor and interpret ATC communications to improve situational awareness.
UA.V.B.K3	Runway markings and signage.
UA.V.B.K4	Traffic patterns used by manned aircraft pilots.
UA.V.B.K5	Security Identification Display Areas (SIDA).
UA.V.B.K6	Sources for airport data.
UA.V.B.K6a	a. Aeronautical charts
UA.V.B.K6b	b. Chart Supplements
UA.V.B.K7	Avoiding bird and wildlife hazards and reporting collisions between aircraft and wildlife.
UA.V.B.K8	Airport and seaplane base lighting.
Risk Management	*[Reserved]*
Skills	*[Not Applicable]*

V. Operations

Task C. Emergency Procedures

References	*AC 107-2; FAA-H-8083-25; FAA-G-8082-22; SAFOs 09013, 10017, 15010*
Objective	*To determine that the applicant is knowledgeable in sUAS emergency procedures.*
Knowledge	*The applicant demonstrates understanding of:*
UA.V.C.K1	Emergency planning and communication.
UA.V.C.K2	Characteristics and potential hazards of lithium batteries.
UA.V.C.K2a	a. Safe transportation such as proper inspection and handling
UA.V.C.K2b	b. Safe charging
UA.V.C.K2c	c. Safe usage
UA.V.C.K2d	d. Risks of fires involving lithium batteries
UA.V.C.K3	Loss of aircraft control link and fly-aways.
UA.V.C.K4	Loss of Global Positioning System (GPS) signal during flight and potential consequences.
UA.V.C.K5	Frequency spectrums and associated limitations.
UA.V.C.K6	Procedures for operations over people.
UA.V.C.K7	Procedures for operations at night.
Risk Management	*[Reserved]*
Skills	*[Not Applicable]*

V. Operations

Task D. Aeronautical Decision-Making

References	*AC 107-2; FAA-H-8083-2, FAA-H-8083-25; FAA-G-8082-22*
Objective	*To determine that the applicant is knowledgeable in aeronautical decision-making.*
Knowledge	*The applicant demonstrates understanding of:*
UA.V.D.K1	Aeronautical decision-making (ADM).
UA.V.D.K1a	a. Effective team communication
UA.V.D.K1b	b. Task management
UA.V.D.K2	Crew Resource Management (CRM).
UA.V.D.K3	Situational awareness.
UA.V.D.K4	Hazardous attitudes.
UA.V.D.K5	Hazard identification and risk assessment.
Risk Management	*[Reserved]*
Skills	*[Not Applicable]*

V. Operations

Task E. Physiology

References	*AC 107-2; FAA-H-8083-2, FAA-H-8083-25; FAA-G-8082-22*
Objective	*To determine that the applicant is knowledgeable in the physiological factors affecting remote pilot performance.*
Knowledge	*The applicant demonstrates understanding of:*
UA.V.E.K1	Physiological considerations and their effects on safety such as dehydration and heatstroke.
UA.V.E.K2	Drug and alcohol use.
UA.V.E.K3	Prescription and over-the-counter medication.
UA.V.E.K4	Hyperventilation.
UA.V.E.K5	Stress and fatigue.
UA.V.E.K6	Factors affecting vision.
UA.V.E.K7	Fitness for flight.
UA.V.E.K8	Physiological aspects of night operation.
UA.V.E.K9	Night illusions.
Risk Management	*[Reserved]*
Skills	*[Not Applicable]*

V. Operations

Task F. Maintenance and Inspection Procedures

References	*AC 107-2; FAA-H-8083-25; FAA-G-8082-22*
Objective	*To determine that the applicant is knowledgeable in sUAS maintenance and inspection procedures.*
Knowledge	*The applicant demonstrates understanding of:*
UA.V.F.K1	Basic maintenance.
UA.V.F.K2	Preflight inspection.
UA.V.F.K3	Techniques to mitigate mechanical failures of all elements used in sUAS operations such as the battery and any device(s) used to operate the sUAS.
UA.V.F.K4	Appropriate record keeping.
UA.V.F.K5	Persons that may perform maintenance on an sUAS.
UA.V.F.K6	Preflight inspection for night operations.
UA.V.F.K7	Manufacturer's Declaration of Compliance for Category 2 and 3 operations.
Risk Management	*[Reserved]*
Skills	*[Not Applicable]*

Appendix Table of Contents

Appendix 1: Certification Knowledge Test, Eligibility, and Testing Centers

Certification Knowledge Test Description

The certification knowledge test is an important part of the airman certification process. Applicants who do not meet the requirements in 14 CFR part 107, section 107.61(d)(2) must pass the knowledge test before applying for a Remote Pilot Certificate with an sUAS rating.

The certification knowledge test consists of objective, multiple-choice questions. There is a single correct response for each test question. Each test question is independent of other questions. A correct response to one question does not depend upon, or influence, the correct response to another. The knowledge test applicant has up to two hours to complete the test.

UAS Topics	Percentage of Items on Test
I. Regulations	15-25%
II. Airspace & Requirements	15-25%
III. Weather	11-16%
IV. Loading & Performance	7-11%
V. Operations	35-45%
Total Number of Questions	**60**

Aviation English Language Standard

In accordance with the requirements of 14 CFR part 107, section 107.61(b) and the FAA English Language Standard for an FAA Certificate Issued Under 14 CFR parts 61, 63, 65, and 107 (AC 60-28, as amended), throughout the application and testing process, the applicant must demonstrate the ability to read, write, speak, and understand the English language. However, the FAA may make an exception if the person is unable to meet one of these requirements due to medical reasons, such as a hearing impairment.

Knowledge Test Requirements

To verify your eligibility to take the certification knowledge test, you must meet the following in accordance with 14 CFR part 107, section 107.67:

- In order for an applicant to take the certification knowledge test, they must be at least 14 years of age; and
- Proper identification is provided, which contains the applicant's:

  - Photograph;
  - Signature;
  - Date of birth; and
  - If the permanent mailing address is a post office box number, then the applicant must provide a current residential address.

To register for any Airman Knowledge Test, an applicant needs to obtain an FAA Tracking Number (FTN). Applicants create an account on the Integrated Airman Certification and Rating Application (IACRA) web page in order to obtain an FTN. Reference this video for instructions about creating an IACRA account:

A list of acceptable documents used to provide proper identification can be found in Advisory Circular (AC) 61-65, Certification: Pilots and Flight and Ground Instructors (as amended).

https://www.youtube.com/watch?v=ETLsH8BruBM.

For the most current Airman Knowledge Testing General Requirements, refer to the FAA Knowledge Testing Applicant Identification, Information Verification, & Authorization Requirements Matrix:

https://www.faa.gov/training_testing/testing/media/testing_matrix.pdf.

Achieving a score of 70% or better is required to be considered as satisfactory for passing the certification knowledge test for a Remote Pilot Certificate with an sUAS rating.

Retaking the sUAS certification knowledge test after a failure involves the following:

- 14 CFR part 107, section 107.71 specifies that an applicant who fails the knowledge test may not retake that knowledge test for 14 calendar days from the date of the previous failure.
- An applicant retesting **after failure** is required to submit the applicable AKTR indicating failure to the airman knowledge testing center prior to retesting.
- No instructor endorsement or other form of written authorization is required to retest after failure.

Airman Knowledge Testing Centers

The FAA's testing vendor, PSI Services, LLC, operates hundreds of testing centers that offer a full range of airman knowledge tests. For information on authorized airman knowledge testing centers and to register, schedule, and pay for the knowledge test, visit https://faa.psiexams.com/faa/login.

Knowledge Test Registration

You may complete registration online, or you may use the link provided above to obtain the contact number for PSI, LLC customer service and register over the phone. In either case, you choose a testing center, and make financial arrangements for test payment. You may **register** for test(s) several weeks in advance, and you may cancel in accordance with the testing center's cancellation policy.

Appendix 2: Knowledge Test Procedures and Tips

Before starting the actual test, the testing center provides an opportunity to practice navigating through the test. This practice or tutorial session may include sample questions to familiarize the applicant with the look and feel of the software (e.g., selecting an answer, marking a question for later review, monitoring time remaining for the test, and other features of the testing software).

The applicant may use certain aids, reference materials, and test materials, as long as the material conforms to the following criteria and does not include actual test questions or answers:

Acceptable Materials	Unacceptable Materials	Notes
Supplement book provided by proctor	Written materials that are handwritten, printed, or electronic	Testing centers may provide calculators and/or deny the use of personal calculators.
All models of aviation-oriented calculators or small electronic calculators that perform only arithmetic functions	Electronic calculators incorporating permanent or continuous type memory circuits without erasure capability	The proctor may prohibit the use of any calculator if he or she is unable to determine the calculator's erasure capability
Calculators with simple programmable memories, which allow addition to, subtraction from, or retrieval of one number from the memory; or simple functions, such as square root and percentages	Magnetic Cards, magnetic tapes, modules, computer chips, or any other device upon which prewritten programs or information related to the test can be stored and retrieved	Applicants surrender printouts of data at the completion of the test if the calculator incorporates this design feature
Scales, straightedges, protractors, plotters, navigation computers, blank log sheets, holding pattern entry aids, and electronic or mechanical calculators that are directly related to the test	Dictionaries	Before, and upon completion of the test, while in the presence of the Unit Member, actuate the ON/OFF switch or RESET button, and perform any other function that ensures erasure of any data stored in memory circuits
Manufacturer's permanently inscribed instructions on the front and back of such aids, e.g., formulas, conversions, regulations, signals, weather data, holding pattern diagrams, frequencies, weight and balance formulas, and air traffic control procedures	Any booklet or manual containing instructions related to use of test aids	The proctor makes the final determination regarding aids, reference materials, and test materials

Test Tips

When taking a knowledge test, please keep the following points in mind:

1. Carefully read the instructions provided with the test.
2. Answer each question in accordance with the latest regulations and guidance publications.
3. Read each question carefully before looking at the answer options. You should clearly understand the problem before trying to solve it.
4. After formulating a response, determine which answer option corresponds with your answer. The answer you choose should completely solve the problem.
5. Remember that only one answer is complete and correct. The other possible answers are either incomplete or erroneous.
6. If a certain question is difficult for you, mark it for review and return to it after you have answered the less difficult questions. This procedure enables you to use the available time to maximum advantage.
7. When solving a calculation problem, be sure to read all the associated notes.
8. For questions involving use of a graph, you may request a printed copy that you can mark in computing your answer. This copy and all other notes and paperwork are given to the testing center upon completion of the test.

Cheating or Other Unauthorized Conduct

To avoid test compromise, computer testing centers follow security procedures described in FAA Order 8080.6 (as amended), *Conduct of Airman Knowledge Tests*. Testing centers terminate a test at any time a test unit member suspects cheating or unauthorized conduct as described in 14 CFR section 61.37.

The FAA investigates and, if the agency determines that cheating or unauthorized conduct has occurred, any airman certificate or rating you hold may be revoked. You are also prohibited from applying for or taking any test for a certificate or rating under 14 CFR part 107, section 107.69 for a period of one year.

Requests for Special Accommodations

An applicant may request approval to take an airman knowledge test with special accommodations. Reasonable accommodations, for testing applicants with disabilities, may be provided, in compliance with applicable law, including the Rehabilitation Act of 1973, and the Americans with Disabilities Act of 1990 (additional information is available at: www.section508.gov).

The applicant's request should include:

- a copy of medical documentation, including the diagnosing physician's name and contact information, verifying the applicant has a learning or reading disability; and

- the requested method of test administration.

Exemptions from 14 CFR

The following applies to requests for special accommodations if the applicant is unable to meet the eligibility requirements of 14 CFR:

- An applicant not meeting regulatory requirements may submit a petition for exemption, from any 14 CFR regulation, in accordance with 14 CFR part 11.

- FAA field offices do not issue exemptions. Applicants should follow the instructions regarding the process for filing a petition, as described in 14 CFR part 11, section 11.63, found here: https://www.faa.gov/regulations_policies/rulemaking/petition/.

Appendix 3: Airman Knowledge Test Report for Certification

Applying for a Remote Pilot Certificate with an sUAS Rating

Immediately upon completion of the certification knowledge test, the applicant receives a printed Airman Knowledge Test Report (AKTR) documenting the score. The applicant should retain the original AKTR.

When applying for a Remote Pilot Certificate with an sUAS rating, the AKTR with passing results is valid for 24 calendar months.

For tests taken prior to January 13, 2020, to obtain a replacement AKTR, the applicant should include a check or money order payable to the FAA in the amount of $12.00 and mail the request to:

Federal Aviation Administration
Airmen Certification Branch, AFB-720
P.O. Box 25082
Oklahoma City, OK 73125

To obtain a copy of the application form or a list of the information required, please see the Airmen Certification Branch webpage at https://www.faa.gov/licenses_certificates/airmen_certification/test_results_replacement/.

For tests taken on or after January 13, 2020, AKTRs may be reprinted from https://faa.psiexams.com/faa/login.

FAA Knowledge Test Question Coding

Each Task in the ACS includes an ACS code. ACS codes are displayed on the AKTR to indicate what Task element was proven deficient on the knowledge test.

Element codes in the ACS divide into four components. For example:

UA.I.B.K10:
- **UA** = ACS (Unmanned Aircraft Systems)
- **I** = Area of Operation (Regulations)
- **B** = Task (Operating Rules)
- **K10** = Knowledge Element (Visual line of sight (VLOS) aircraft operations.)

How to Obtain the Remote Pilot Certificate

To obtain a Remote Pilot Certificate with an sUAS rating, choose one of the processes described below (from 14 CFR part 107).

- Part 61 pilot certificate holders with a current flight review may follow any process.
- If you are not a part 61 certificated pilot that has completed a flight review in the preceding 24 calendar months, then choose from the two columns on the left.

Visit the References chapter in AC 107-2, Small Unmanned Aircraft Systems (sUAS) (as amended) to review more information about each process.

AC 107-2 sUAS		Part 61 Pilot Certificate Holders with a Current Flight Review	
Online Application After Knowledge Test [1]	**Paper Application [2] After Knowledge Test [1]**	**Online Application After Online Course**	**Paper Application [2] After Online Course**
Submit an online application using Integrated Airman Certification and/or Rating Application (IACRA.)	Complete FAA Form 8710-13 and mail it with the original copy of your Knowledge Test Report to: *DOT/FAA* *Airmen Certification Branch* *PO Box 25082* *Oklahoma City, OK 73125*	Submit an online application using IACRA. Meet with an FAA-authorized individual [3] to validate your: • IACRA application ID number • FAA Tracking Number (FTN) • Identification • Online course completion certificate • Pilot certificate • Flight review documentation	Complete FAA Form 8710-13. Meet with an FAA-authorized individual [3] to validate your: • FAA Form 8710-13 • Identification • Online course completion certificate • Pilot certificate • Flight review documentation
Receive email notification to print and sign a temporary certificate through IACRA.	Do not receive a temporary certificate.	Receive a temporary certificate in person (or if meeting with a Certificated Flight Instructor (CFI), receive email notification to print and sign a temporary certificate through IACRA). [4]	Receive a temporary certificate in person (except when meeting with a CFI) [4]
Receive a permanent certificate by mail.	Receive a permanent certificate by mail.	Receive a permanent certificate by mail.	Receive a permanent certificate by mail.

Notes:

[1] *If you successfully complete the FAA UAG Knowledge Test, you are not required to meet with an FAA-authorized individual because your identity is established at an AKTC.*

[2] *Paper applications delay issuance of a permanent certificate because the application is verified and processed by the FAA-authorized individual, FSDO, and Airman Registry.*

[3] *An FAA-authorized individual may be a Certificated Flight Instructor (CFI), an Airman Certification Representative (ACR) for a pilot school, a person designated by a FSDO, or a Remote Pilot Examiner (RPE).*

[4] *CFIs can assist in the processing of applications and can facilitate issuance of a temporary certificate through IACRA, but cannot directly issue a temporary certificate when IACRA is not used.*

Appendix 4: References

This ACS is based on the following 14 CFR parts, FAA guidance documents, and other documents.

Reference	Title
14 CFR part 47	Aircraft Registration
14 CFR part 48	Registration and Marking Requirements for Small Unmanned Aircraft
14 CFR part 61	Certification: Pilots, Flight Instructors, and Ground Instructors
14 CFR part 71	Designation of Class A, B, C, D, and E Airspace Areas; Air Traffic Service Routes; and Reporting Points
14 CFR part 89	Remote Identification (RID)
14 CFR part 107	Small Unmanned Aircraft Systems (sUAS)
AC 00-6	Aviation Weather
AC 60-28	FAA English Language Standard for an FAA Certificate Issued Under 14 CFR Parts 61, 63, 65, and 107
AC 107-2	Small Unmanned Aircraft Systems (sUAS)
AC 150/5200-32	Reporting Wildlife Aircraft Strikes
AIM	Aeronautical Information Manual
FAA-H-8083-2	Risk Management Handbook
FAA-H-8083-25	Pilot's Handbook of Aeronautical Knowledge
FAA-G-8082-22	Remote Pilot – Small Unmanned Aircraft Systems Study Guide
SAFO 09013	Fighting Fires Caused by Lithium Type Batteries in Portable Electronic Devices
SAFO 10015	Flying in the Wire Environment
SAFO 10017	Risks in Transporting Lithium Batteries in Cargo by Aircraft
SAFO 15010	Carriage of Spare Lithium Batteries in Carry-on and Checked Baggage

Note: *Users should reference the current edition of the reference documents listed above. Safety Alerts for Operators (SAFOs) and the current edition of all FAA publications is located at* www.faa.gov.

Appendix 5: Abbreviations and Acronyms

Abbreviation or Acronym	Definition
14 CFR	Title 14 of the Code of Federal Regulations
AC	Advisory Circular
ACR	Airman Certification Representative
ACS	Airman Certification Standards
ADM	Aeronautical Decision-Making
AELS	Aviation English Language Standard
AFS	Flight Standards Service
AIM	Aeronautical Information Manual
AKTC	Airman Knowledge Testing Center
AKTR	Airman Knowledge Test Report
ASOS	Automated Surface Observation System
ATC	Air Traffic Control
ATIS	Automatic Terminal Information Service
AWOS	Automated Weather Observation System
CFI	Certificated Flight Instructor
CRM	Crew Resource Management
CTAF	Common Traffic Advisory Frequency
DOT	Department of Transportation
FAA	Federal Aviation Administration
FSDO	Flight Standards District Office
FTN	FAA Tracking Number
GPS	Global Positioning System
IACRA	Integrated Airman Certification and Rating Application
METAR	Aviation Routine Weather Reports (Meteorological Aerodrome Report)
MTR	Military Training Routes
NAS	National Airspace System
NOTAM	Notice to Airmen
NSA	National Security Areas
ODA	Organization Designation Authorization
PIC	Pilot-in-Command
RPE	Remote Pilot Examiner

Abbreviation or Acronym	Definition
SAFO	Safety Alert for Operators
SIDA	Security Identification Display Area
SMS	Safety Management System
sUAS	Small Unmanned Aircraft System
TAF	Terminal Area Forecast
TFR	Temporary Flight Restrictions
TRSA	Terminal Radar Service Area
UAS	Unmanned Aircraft Systems
UNICOM	Aeronautical Advisory Communication Station
VFR	Visual Flight Rules
VLOS	Visual Line of Sight